Wild flower walks

Yorkshire Dales

SOUTHERN REGION

C000076205

WATERFRONT

Amanda and Brin Best

ISBN 0-946184-98-4

British Library Cataloguing-in-Publication Data
A catalogue entry for this book is available from the British Library

Copyright © Text and photographs Amanda and Brin Best/Kingfisher Productions, 2002

Maps reproduced from Ordnance Survey mapping on behalf of The Controller of Her Majesty's Stationery Office © Crown Copyright. Licence Number MC 100039367

All rights reserved. This book is sold subject to the condition that it shall not, by way of trade or otherwise, be lent, hired out, re-sold or otherwise circulated in any form without the publisher's prior consent. No part of this publication may be reproduced or transmitted in any form or by any means, electronic or mechanical, including photocopying, recording or any information storage or retrieval system, without the prior permission in writing from the publisher or a licence, permitting restricted copying.

Published by Waterfront
A division of Kingfisher Productions
The Dalesmade Centre
Watershed Mill
Settle
North Yorkshire
BD24 9LR

Design by Innovation *for* Education

Printed and bound in the UK by The Amadeus Press, Cleckheaton, West Yorkshire

Cover photograph: Upper Wharfedale

Contents

Introduction

THE YORKSHIRE DALES are recognised as one of Britain's foremost areas for wild flowers. The varied upland habitats, ranging from pristine hay meadows to exposed limestone pavements, support hundreds of different plant species, including many rare and local species difficult to find elsewhere in the country. This, coupled with the beautiful landscape and fascinating industrial and agricultural history of the region, make it a superb place for plant hunting.

This book takes you on guided walks through ten of the best areas for wild flowers in the Dales. From the river valleys to the high peaks, we have chosen walks that will guarantee a wide range of typical Dales flowers, together with most of the specialities. Our main aim in writing the book is to encourage interest in wild flowers and their conservation. To this end we have included walks that will enable you to see all the main habitats within the southern region of Airedale, Ribblesdale and Wharfedale, with details of over 180 different flowers to look for along the way. All the walks pass through land protected in some way for its nature conservation interest, be that as part of a reserve or linked to agri-environment schemes. Most pass through areas which have been designated Sites of Special Scientific Interest by the government.

The walks are at most five and a half miles in length, to allow you sufficient time to enjoy the flowers along the way. They are almost all gentle to moderate routes, so that as many people as possible can enjoy them. Although you will see many scarce and unusual species on the walks, the book does not take you to all the rarities. Many of these are sensitive to disturbance and grow in locations which are remote and difficult to reach. We have left them alone.

Although always following footpaths, many of the walks are in wild country, away from the principal walking routes. Indeed, we tried to avoid the well-trodden routes which need a rest from the thousands of feet that pound them every season. Whilst on the walks your safety is paramount, so take due account of the information in the factfiles that accompany each walk to judge their suitability for you. Also be aware of your impact on the places you will visit, and observe the Country Code (printed on page 57) at all times.

There are many pressures on Britain's botanical

heritage, and the Yorkshire Dales have not escaped in this respect. Recreation activities, land use changes and intensive farming methods are all very real threats to many of the wild flowers you will see on the walks. By buying this book you are also helping to protect the wild flowers of the Dales, as a donation will be made from each book sold towards conservation activities in the region.

Although we have chosen these walks for their wild flower interest, they are enjoyable at any time of year. They are all in very scenic locations and some are at their most dramatic in winter. In the factfiles we have indicated the best months to visit them for their wild flowers.

We hope you will enjoy these walks as much as we have over the years, and that the weather will be fine on your visits. Happy plant hunting!

Amanda and Brin Best
Otley, October 2002

A legend for the maps which appear in the main text is shown at the back of the book

The walks

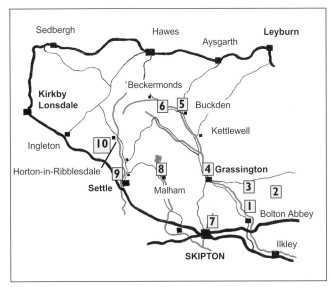

1. Strid Wood
2. Trollers Gill
3. Grassington
4. Grass Wood
5. Buckden
6. Langstrothdale
7. Skipton Wood
8. Malham Tarn
9. Langcliffe Scars
10. Ingleborough

Walk 1

Strid Wood

The wooded valley of the river Wharfe above Bolton Abbey provides the backdrop for this delightful walk. The route takes you through woodland which has been declared a Site of Special Scientific Interest, amid a landscape that inspired Turner and Wordsworth. You will also witness the awe of the dramatic and treacherous section of the Wharfe known as the 'Strid'.

FACTFILE

Distance: 4.7 mi (7.5 km)

Time needed: 3.5 hours

Starting point: SE 077553

Car parking: Cavendish Pavilion car park, run by the Bolton Abbey estate (£)

Paths: even, partly surfaced

Gradients: gentle-moderate

Refreshments: Cavendish Pavilion has a cafe and shop

Toilets: Cavendish Pavilion

Public transport: daily bus service between Bolton Abbey and Ilkley (and on to Leeds and Bradford) during the summer

Notes: this is a popular site for day trippers and the section from Cavendish Pavilion to the Strid can be very busy on warm summer days

blue *best flower months*
pink *good flower months*

J F M A M J J A S O N D

HEAD NORTH-WEST from the Bolton Abbey estate car park to the bridge over the Wharfe near the Cavendish Pavilion, where this walks begins. Pass the pavilion and gift shop and go through a gate to join a surfaced track that takes you through the first section of Strid Wood [1]. The wood is the largest in the Yorkshire Dales growing over acid soils, and a very rich flora has developed. The area is also well known for its fungi, bird and mammal life, making a visit throughout the year rewarding. This, together with the scenic attraction of the Strid and nearby Bolton Priory, lead to high visitor numbers along this section of the walk. Upstream from the Strid, and on the opposite side of the river, there are many fewer visitors.

While in this part of Strid Wood look for **woodruff**, **lords-and-ladies**, **water avens**, **wood avens**, **common figwort**, **ramsons**, **bluebell**, **opposite-leaved golden-saxifrage** and **wood stitchwort**. Keep right at two forks in the path, and carry on through an open area skirting the river to reach the rapids of the Strid [2]. This dramatic feature is formed as the river

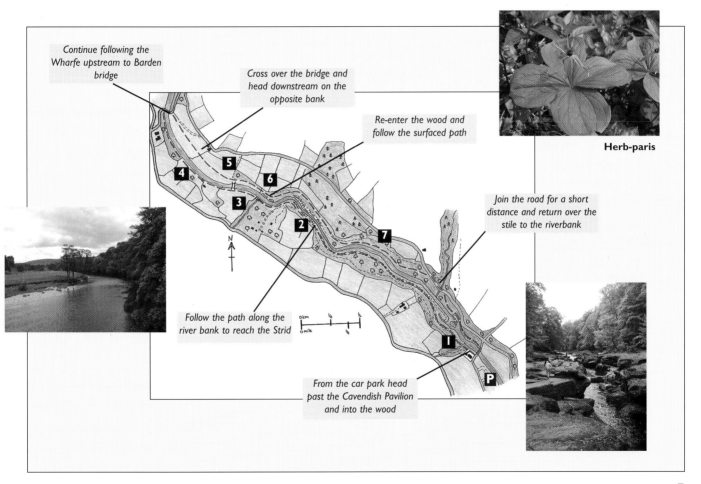

Continue following the Wharfe upstream to Barden bridge

Cross over the bridge and head downstream on the opposite bank

Re-enter the wood and follow the surfaced path

Herb-paris

Join the road for a short distance and return over the stile to the riverbank

Follow the path along the river bank to reach the Strid

From the car park head past the Cavendish Pavilion and into the wood

4

5

6

3

2

7

1

P

N

0 km   ⅛   ¼
0 mile   ⅛

Wharfe narrows to a few metres in width. The entire water column is forced to pass through this narrow channel, which has over the years eroded the river bed 20 m down into the limestone. The Strid has claimed many lives over the years, its name referring to the 'stride' thought necessary to cross the channel at this point. Only fools have tried this and most have not lived to tell the tale. Examine the pools of standing water at the edge of the Strid, where crayfish are sometimes seen.

Continue on past the Strid on the lower path, ignoring a sign to 'Strid Car Park and Barden'. Excellent

views of the river are possible along this next stretch of the walk, with considerable bird interest, including regular dipper, kingfisher and goosander. Soon you leave the wood via a wooden footbridge over Barden beck, and the riverside path takes you through some damp pastures with much botanical interest [3]. Among the flowers growing here are **common spotted-orchid**, **great burnet**, **greater bird's-foot-trefoil**, **meadow crane's-bill**, **yellow rattle**, **quaking grass**, **meadow vetchling** and **marsh hawk's-beard**.

Pass the stone aqueduct and continue upstream towards a woodland. A wet area part way along this path contains **monkeyflower**, **water forget-me-not**, **brook-lime**, **water-cress**, **marsh-marigold**, **marsh thistle** and **ragged-robin** [4]. Cross over the river at Barden bridge and follow the path on the opposite side of the river, heading downstream. The path first heads through an area of grazed fields with few flowers. The river has caused serious erosion problems here and the bank is unstable and undercut in several places. A little further on an area of grassland supports a range of species not seen before on this walk, including **tormentil**, **heath bedstraw**, **heath speedwell**, **pignut**, **devils'-bit scabious** and **common ragwort**.

You then enter the area of Strid Wood on the opposite side of the river to the section you started in. Here there are many oak and **beech** trees, and beneath a rich flora [6] can be found. Among the many species growing here are **greater stitchwort, snowdrop, sanicle, wood-sorrel, wood anemone, dog's mercury, red campion, bitter vetch, wood sage** and **foxglove. Common cow-wheat** also grows in this area, its tubular yellow flowers growing from within wing-like pairs of leaves. Cows that grazed on the plant were said to produce splendid yellow butter. Follow the path as it climbs away from the river and you will reach an area with fine views of the Strid from above. Streams tumble down the hillside past the path, and these are excellent places to look for plants which prefer damp conditions such as **opposite-leaved golden-saxifrage**, horsetails and ferns such as **hard fern**.

Continue on the main path, bearing right to descend towards the river again. As the wood broadens out there are many new species to look for, among them **enchanter's-nightshade, hedge woundwort, creeping jenny** and **primrose**. An unusual grass, **wood melick**, also grows in this area. The path then hugs the riverbank, providing access to some damp areas of woodland with many additional species [7]. Here there is **butterbur, meadowsweet, lesser stitchwort, wood crane's-bill, ground-elder** and the distinctive **herb-paris**.

Join the road for a short section, then head down towards the riverbank again over a stile, pausing in May to look for the scarce **toothwort** either side of the path.

This parasitic plant is quite unlike any other British species, pale flesh in colour with its stem bearing several flowers, all turned to one side of the inflorescence. Toothwort's preferred host plant is **hazel**, which grows quite commonly in Strid Wood. It usually grows in clumps around the roots of the host tree and attaches pad-like suckers to these, eventually diverting the sap for its own use. Its name is thought to derive from the tooth-shaped flowers and leaves.

Follow the path through an area of improved grassland by the river and proceed on to the wooden bridge. On the other side of the bridge you can see the Cavendish Pavilion, which was originally built in the 1890s as a tea room for visitors. Continue over the bridge to where your walk began. ☙

Other wildlife

Strid Wood is an important site for **birds**, with the highest breeding density of pied flycatchers in the Dales. These take advantage of nest boxes put up by the estate staff. Wood warblers and redstarts also nest in the wood. Along the river there are many dippers, which share this clean stretch of the Wharfe with goosander, grey wagtail, common sandpiper and kingfisher. Look for woodpeckers in mature trees, and at dusk the courtship flight of woodcock, like a giant snipe. Many **fungi** species occur in the wood in the autumn, including a number of scarce and local species.

Walk 2

Trollers Gill

A short but spectacular walk which takes you through the dramatic limestone gorge of Trollers Gill, home to many interesting plants and rumoured to provide shelter for trolls. Visitors in June and July will be greeted by carpets of common rock-rose, and can venture into the depths of the gorge to find flowers clinging to the rocks of this unusual landform.

FACTFILE

Distance: 2.3 mi (3.7 km)

Time needed: 2 hours

Starting point: SE 067609

Parking: on roadside just before the bridge at Parcevall Hall, or in the hall car park, but only if visiting the gardens (£)

Paths: very varied; includes boulder-strewn section

Gradients: mostly gentle, but with a moderate climb

Refreshments: tea room at Parcevall Hall in summer months

Toilets: no public toilets nearby

Public transport: nearest bus stop Grassington

Notes: Parcevall Hall gardens are open Easter to 31 October, 10:00-18:00 daily (£)

blue *best flower months*
pink *good flower months*

J F M A M J J A S O N D

AT THE entrance to Parcevall Hall leave the road through the gate near the bridge onto the footpath signed 'Gill Heads and New Road'. Follow the bank of Skyreholme Beck along the rushy pasture, through a second gate, and over a small gated stile. Note the streamside trees [1] which are almost all **alder**, with just a few **ash** and **sycamore**. Alder thrives in wet ground but is now found less often due to the drainage of wetlands and the spreading fungal alder disease which is believed to be carried in water. Note the small brown cones which stay on the alder tree all year round.

Remnants of woodland flora survive under the trees on the river bank including **dog's mercury**, **hedge woundwort** and **herb-robert**.

Carry on through the pasture to the barn. Flowers you will see here are generally the common agricultural weeds of pasture, including **common ragwort**, **creeping buttercup**, **creeping thistle** and **spear thistle**, but a closer look near the wall and beck will reveal others [2]. **Lady's-mantle** and **common knapweed** occur, with **tormentil** and **heath bedstraw** in pockets of more acidic grassland. Shady areas under

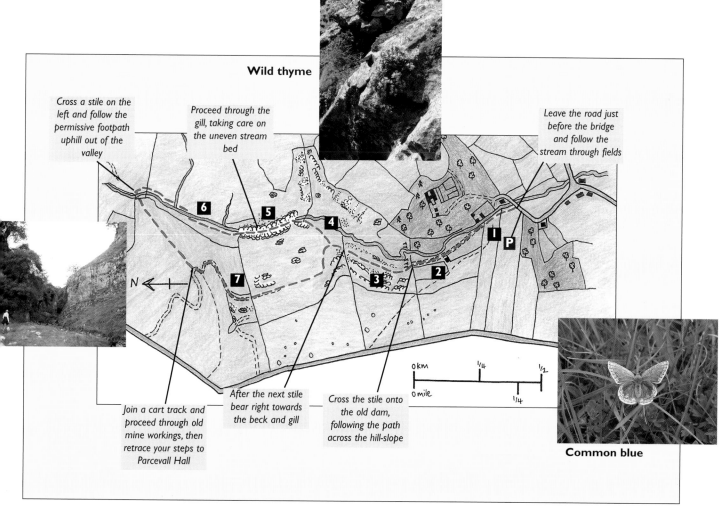

Wild thyme

Cross a stile on the left and follow the permissive footpath uphill out of the valley

Proceed through the gill, taking care on the uneven stream bed

Leave the road just before the bridge and follow the stream through fields

6

5

4

1 P

N

7

3

2

Join a cart track and proceed through old mine workings, then retrace your steps to Parcevall Hall

After the next stile bear right towards the beck and gill

Cross the stile onto the old dam, following the path across the hill-slope

0km   ¼   ½
0 mile   ¼

Common blue

11

the trees support odd **bluebells** and **common dog-violets**. Cross over the stile onto the old dam structure which once held water to supply a mill further down the valley. The dam was never reinstated after it burst in 1899 and Skyreholme Beck now meanders tortuously where the reservoir would have filled the valley. Follow the path through the **bracken**-covered slopes.

The path soon crosses a slope where wild flowers are brought to eye level on rocky outcrops [3]. Among these natural rock-gardens grow **wild thyme, common rock-rose, salad burnet, biting stonecrop, fairy flax** and **dove's-foot crane's-bill**. Also worth noting are the ferns such as **maidenhair spleenwort** and some of the unusual large, leaf-like lichens. In places **common rock-rose** abounds on the slope in small mounds, its yellow tissue-paper flowers catching easily in the breeze. From this slope are good views across the valley to the steep hillsides of Old Man's Scar and Nape Scar, where **yew** trees grow high on the cliffs, dark against the pale limestone rocks.

Follow the path over the stile in the wall but instead of bearing left in the direction of the public footpath sign, go right parallel to the route of the beck. The clear, lime-rich waters of the beck and nearby spring support large beds of the white-flowered **water-cress** [4]. **Water mint** and **meadowsweet** grow among the rushes in the damp area between the beck and the spring. Look out

too for **greater bird's-foot trefoil, yarrow, meadow vetchling** and **eyebright** among the taller grass. More scattered **alder** trees favour the damp conditions.

The steep hill-slope near the spring, with its patches of limestone scree, is another place to look for those natural rock-garden flowers. As well as the species mentioned above, you will find **lady's-bedstraw, quaking grass, crosswort, mouse-ear hawkweed** and **herb-robert**.

Proceed over the next stile and into the mouth of Trollers Gill [5]. This small gorge was cut by the erosive force of water gradually eating into the limestone rock. Overhanging cliffs remain, with large fallen boulders strewn along their bases. Local folklore tells of trolls who

roll these rocks down from overhead, and also of a ghostly hound that haunts the shady caves. Indeed the gill can feel eerie in its stillness and shade, even on a bright windy day.

The stream-bed is usually dry here now, but take time and care over the uneven rocks. Stop to look for **harebell, marjoram, wall lettuce, field scabious, wood-sage** and the feathery tufts of **lesser meadow-rue** growing on the cliffs. Among the now familiar **common rock-rose** and **wild thyme** grow **hairy rock-cress, shining crane's-bill, burnet-saxifrage** and **limestone bedstraw**. The shady rock crevaces favour ferns, including **wall-rue** and **brittle bladder-fern**. The bottom of the gill is shaded and dry, mimicking woodland conditions with plants such as **dog's mercury**. Higher on the sides of the gill **yew** trees and other bushes grow.

The path leaves Trollers Gill and follows the route of Skyreholme Beck which is usually flowing again here [6]. Marsh-loving plants grow along the low banks of the stream. Yellow **marsh-marigolds** and pink **ragged-robin** are easily seen when in flower, as are **lesser spearwort** and **cuckooflower**. Search too for the less conspicuous **brooklime** and **common marsh-bedstraw**.

Shortly you will cross a wall and stile on your left, following the route of a permissive path uphill out of the valley. The path crosses rough pasture and soon joins an old, winding cart track. Turn left onto the track and walk down into an area of old mine workings [7]. Here you will see many of the flowers seen before on the limestone rocks and scree, and also the short, yellow **carline thistle**. There are carpets of **red clover** and **white clover** forming a patchy mosaic with the yellow **biting stonecrop**. **Spring sandwort** shows its tiny, white star-like flowers on the old spoil heaps, where it is adapted to living among the high concentration of lead.

As you leave the mine workings the path continues downhill between tall swathes of **bracken** covering the lower slopes. This fern is very vigorous in its growth and little else survives among the dense bracken fronds, except for a few species which tolerate the shady conditions. The path rejoins your original route at the wooden footpath sign. Turn right and retrace your steps back to Parcevall Hall. This religious retreat has impressive gardens which are worth a visit when open to the public during the summer. ✿

Other wildlife

Among the many **bird** species which live around the gill are a large colony of jackdaws, which scold any intruders. Green woodpecker, kestrel, peregrine falcon, little owl and short-eared owl are also present in the area. **Stoats** are common and prey on unsuspecting rabbits.

Walk 3
Grassington

The jewel in the crown of this valley walk is the spectacular wildflower meadow that has survived changes in modern agriculture due to its location at the site of the old Grassington hospital. Elsewhere colourful flower meadows have given way to uniform green grassland, but wildflowers still abound on roadsides, forgotten field corners and on the riverbank.

FACTFILE

Distance: 4.7 mi (7.6 km)

Time needed: 3.5 hours

Starting point: SE 003636

Parking: Yorkshire Dales National Park car park, Grassington (£)

Paths: even, some surfaced (including small section of road)

Gradients: gentle

Refreshments: wide variety in Grassington, pub and shop in Hebden

Toilets: Grassington and Hebden

Public transport: daily bus service between Grassington and Ilkley (and on to Leeds and Bradford) during the summer

Notes: the main meadow is usually cut in mid July

blue *best flower months*
pink *good flower months*

| J | F | M | A | M | J | J | A | S | O | N | D |

FROM THE car park at the National Park Visitor Centre, take the narrow, walled Sedber Lane path to Linton Falls [1]. This old pack-horse trail is lined with **sweet cicely**, **herb-robert**, **oxeye daisy** and **meadow crane's-bill**. **Shining crane's-bill** grows in crannies in the dry stone wall. As you walk past the **sweet cicely**, or crush some of its leaves, you can smell the strong fragrance of aniseed. It is believed that the plant was introduced into Britain for culinary purposes, the strong flavour disguising less fresh ingredients.

Near the Bridge at Linton Falls look out for some of the flowers that enjoy the damp conditions near the River Wharfe. **Monkey flower**, **meadowsweet** and **marsh valerian** can usually be seen. Just before the bridge, take the left-hand stile into the grazed field and follow the footpath parallel to the river. Few flowers survive the intense grazing and it is interesting to note the variety of thistles that the animals have avoided, including **creeping**, **spear** and **welted thistles**. Over the second stile is a small area of exposed limestone that is probably the remains of an earlier river bank, before the water eroded down to its current position. Here

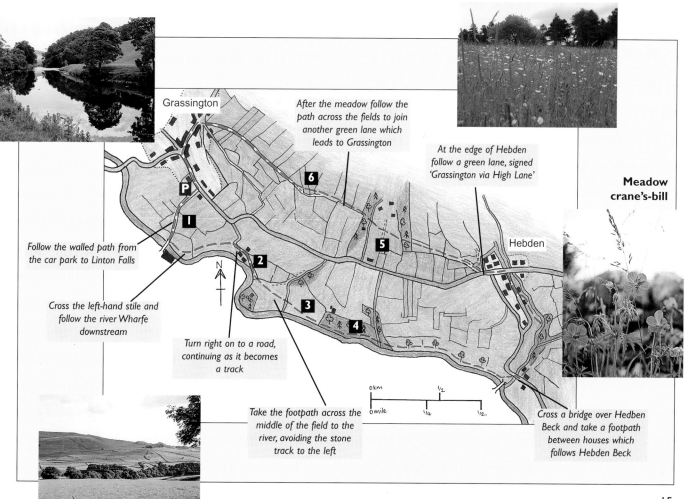

Grassington

After the meadow follow the path across the fields to join another green lane which leads to Grassington

At the edge of Hebden follow a green lane, signed 'Grassington via High Lane'

Meadow crane's-bill

Hebden

P

1

6

5

2

3

4

Follow the walled path from the car park to Linton Falls

Cross the left-hand stile and follow the river Wharfe downstream

Turn right on to a road, continuing as it becomes a track

Take the footpath across the middle of the field to the river, avoiding the stone track to the left

Cross a bridge over Hedben Beck and take a footpath between houses which follows Hebden Beck

N

0km 1/2
0 mile 1/4 1/2

15

mouse-ear hawkweed, wild thyme, black medick and parsley-piert have escaped the sheep.

Shortly the path joins a minor road where you turn right [2]. The roadside verges are colourful with meadow crane's-bill, lady's bedstraw, meadow buttercup, water avens, crosswort, meadow vetchling and common knapweed. In spring you can see the unusual flowers of lords-and-ladies, and later in the year clusters of its bright red poisonous berries. The roots of this plant were collected in Elizabethan times for their high starch content, which was used to stiffen fashionable linen ruffs.

The road passes some houses and deteriorates into a

rough track. Look out along the unmanaged edges of the track for meadow flowers such as yellow rattle. Take the footpath across the middle of the field avoiding the stone farm track on the left. The path soon joins the river bank where you will find quaking grass, betony and common restharrow. Restharrow's name means literally 'to stop the harrow', and in the days of horse-drawn ploughs its matted stems and roots hindered progress considerably. It was also known as wild liquorice, as children in the north dug up the underground stems and chewed them.

At [3] the path crosses a spring where it is worth taking a closer look for some of the water-loving flowers. The large yellow monkeyflower stands out among the patches of water-cress and similar fool's water-cress. Elsewhere there is water mint, devils'-bit scabious, eyebright, common scurvygrass, marsh thistle and great burnet. Wetter areas have the unusual three-lobed leaves and fringed white flowers of bogbean. Higher up are patches of the insectivorous common butterwort and the delicate bird's-eye primrose.

The route now passes along the riverbank shaded by large trees [4], including horse-chestnut with its exotic-looking cream and pink spikes of flowers. Greater knapweed and water forget-me-not can also be found. Howgill Beck flows down a shady wooded gulley, with woodland flora including the garlic-smelling ramsons and **dog's mercury**. At the suspension bridge, take the short footpath on the left up to the road. Follow the road right and turn immediately left after the bridge over Hebden Beck onto the footpath through houses and gardens. The large leaves of **butterbur** grow along the stream-side, the strange pink flowers having withered much earlier in the year before the leaves appeared.

Look out for **damson** trees before the fish farm, then keep following the path beyond it across Hebden Beck and through some fields that have 'Countryside Stewardship' signs. Eventually you reach the road where you turn right and then left onto the main Grassington road. At the edge of the village, past the hotel and the vehicle yard, take the footpath signed 'Grassington via High Lane' which follows a narrow, walled pack-horse trail. Make sure you do not take the vehicle track adjacent to the sheds. The tracksides and unmanaged edges of these fields are places to look for remnants of meadow flowers, including **great burnet** and **field scabious**. The great burnet is an elegant plant with a compact blood-red flower head. For centuries it was used to staunch wounds and as a remedy for internal bleeding, as ancient herbalists believed that plants advertise their medicinal properties through their outward signs.

After crossing the third wall you walk through a narrow plantation with pines and enter the grounds of the old hospital [5]. The buildings have recently been demolished and new houses built, but the grounds remain as a colourful hay meadow. This diverse meadow is one of the best in the county, being designated a Site of Special Scientific Interest. Among the many flowers you will see are **oxeye daisy**, **tufted vetch**, **melancholy thistle**, **meadowsweet**, **bugle**, **meadow buttercup**, **lady's-mantle**, **red clover** and many others including a wide variety of grasses, sedges and rushes.

Follow the stone flag path through the meadow, across the tarmac drive and out into the fields beyond. Pause in these fields to look across the valley where the long, thin, terraced lines of old field patterns called 'lynchets' can be readily seen, especially in the evening sunlight [6]. Here the path hugs the bottom edges of the stone-walled fields and soon joins another walled lane called High Lane which takes you into Grassington.

In Grassington bear left down the hill to the main square, and left on to the main road and back to the visitor centre car park. ❀

Other wildlife

There are many **birds** to look for along the river Wharfe, among them dipper, kingfisher and goosander, a fish-eating duck. Sand martins have made colonies in the sandy river banks above the water, where **trout** and **grayling** live. Little owls are commonly seen in the fields between Hebden and Grassington.

Walk 4

Grass Wood

This short walk takes you through the rich limestone woodland of Grass Wood Nature Reserve to the plateau of open wooded pasture known as Bastow Wood. In May and June a diverse woodland ground flora develops, with carpets of primroses, bluebells and lily-of-the-valley. There is a remarkable range of wildflowers and many hours can be spent enjoying the beautiful flowers and landscape.

FACTFILE

Distance: 3.4 mi (5.4 km)

Time needed: 3 hours

Starting point: SD 985652

Parking: small quarry car park off Grass Wood Lane

Paths: mostly even; some surfaced

Gradients: gentle-moderate, odd steep slopes

Refreshments: wide variety in Grassington

Toilets: Grassington

Public transport: nearest bus stop Grassington

Notes: Grass Wood is a Yorkshire Wildlife Trust reserve and no dogs are allowed

blue *best flower months*
pink *good flower months*

| J | F | M | A | M | J | J | A | S | O | N | D |

THE WALK starts from the small quarry car park hidden behind the roadside wall, just off Grass Wood Lane. Leave the car park from the left-hand stile (with your back to the road) and follow the path to join the main track lined with a wooden fence. Grass Wood is predominantly an **ash** woodland with **hazel** understorey, and here you can see that the hazel has been coppiced [1]. This is a traditional form of management and maintains an open woodland where flowers growing at ground level can thrive in the sunlight let through the canopy. Hidden among the swathes of

bluebell and **dog's mercury** are **water-avens**, **lords-and-ladies**, **bugle**, **wood anemone**, **primrose**, **common dog-violet**, **wild strawberry** and **lady's-mantle**. Look out too for the dark pink flowers of **early-purple orchid**.

This path leads to the edge of the woodland and a large vehicle-sized track and gateway where cut logs are sometimes stored [2]. Follow the track uphill to the right. Between the **beech** trees at the woodland edge you can catch glimpses of the impressive Kilnsey Crag across the bright green pasture-land. Breathe in the

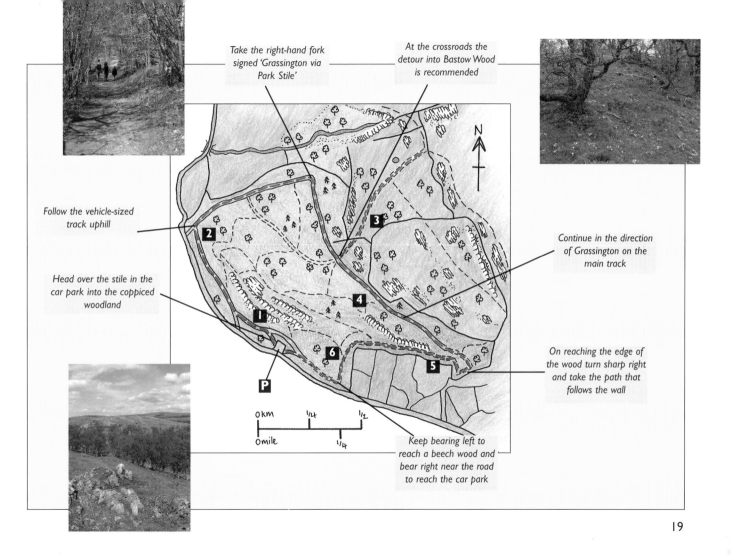

Take the right-hand fork signed 'Grassington via Park Stile'

At the crossroads the detour into Bastow Wood is recommended

Follow the vehicle-sized track uphill

Head over the stile in the car park into the coppiced woodland

Continue in the direction of Grassington on the main track

On reaching the edge of the wood turn sharp right and take the path that follows the wall

Keep bearing left to reach a beech wood and bear right near the road to reach the car park

N

0 km   1/4   1/2
0 mile   1/4

2

3

1

4

6

5

P

smell of the **ramsons** which grows here in profusion. After just under half a mile the path forks. Follow the main track around the sharp right-hand corner sign-posted 'Grassington via Park Stile'. The woodland is quite open here as the Yorkshire Wildlife Trust have been removing the conifer trees in order to restore the natural broadleaf woodland. Later in the season **meadowsweet** and **common valerian** line the path, and **honeysuckle** clambers among the trees.

There are outcrops of limestone pavement here, with trees and plants growing out of the crevices. Such wooded pavement is a very rare habitat nationally, and this is one of the features that makes Grass Wood such an important site.

Shortly you come to a cross-roads with a sign-post. The circular walk carries straight on but a detour to Bastow Wood Site of Special Scientific Interest is recommended. Follow the path to the left looking out for a **bird cherry** tree with its mass of white flower spikes in May. Cross over the wall at the stile and immediately on your right is a bank with the delicate pink flowers of **bird's-eye primrose.** You are now in Bastow Wood [3]. A well-trodden path passes through this area of ancient grassland with its scattered and contorted trees. In May the path is lined with carpets of **primroses, cowslips** and violets. In later months you will find **devils'-bit scabious, common rock-rose** and **salad burnet.** Near an old dew-

pond at the left of the path you can generally find the open yellow face of **mountain pansy**. On the dried out pond itself look for **barren strawberry** and the tiny **rue-leaved saxifrage**. Explore further and you will be rewarded with other interesting species, including **early-purple orchid, bloody crane's-bill** and **dropwort**.

Retrace your steps back to the crossroads, and carry on the main track in the direction of Grassington, passing the Brigantian Fort Gregory, now a ruin. The path narrows, leading downhill between steep banks covered with mossy boulders and masses of **lily-of-the-valley [4]**. Stoop down to take a closer look at the flowers

and take in the attractive scent. You will also find **wood-sorrel**, **ground-ivy**, **lesser celandine** and **crosswort** here. The unusual **herb-paris** also grows in this area of the wood. It is quite unlike any other native plant, with a parasol-like whorl of four broad leaves and a single central green flower. It is poisonous and pollinated by carrion flies which are attracted by its slightly unpleasant smell. Another unusual but typical woodland species found in this locality is **goldilocks buttercup**.

The footpath takes you to the boundary wall of the wood where there is a stile. Immediately before the stile turn sharp right and follow the wall-side path along the edge of the wood [5]. The open woodland edges support some flowers more typical of the pasture land, including **meadow crane's-bill** and **pignut**. Elsewhere the typical woodland flowers of **bluebell**, **dog's mercury**, **red campion**, **lesser celandine** and **ramsons** abound, together with **white campion**. If you missed the **herb-paris** earlier hunt for it here under a white-flowering **bird cherry** tree. There are numerous small pathways through the woodland here which can lead to confusion. Keep bearing left, with the rocky cliff of Dewbottom Scar glimpsed through the trees up to your right and you will soon see a gateway to the road through the beech trees. This **beech** woodland is planted and not natural to the Yorkshire Dales [6]. The dense leaf canopy lets little light through and few plants grow among the thick layer of beech leaves on the ground. In the autumn many species of fungi grow here, including several very scarce species, making Grass Wood one of the best sites in the Dales for mycologists.

Turn sharply to the right on a path that runs more or less parallel to the road. Just after this turn is a small hollow on the right with **solomon's-seal**, although this may be a garden escape. Elsewhere in the wood the rare **angular solomon's-seal** grows on limestone scree in one of its few Yorkshire sites.

Where the path forks, take the upper right-hand path which carries on at the same level rather than dipping down to the road. Along the fenced section of walk you will be able to see the quarry car park on the left. Follow the small track down over the stile into the car park. ✿

Other wildlife

Grass Wood is a fine site for woodland **birds**, supporting several uncommon species. These include pied flycatcher, wood warbler and redstart, which occur among larger numbers of commoner warblers and titmice. Green and great-spotted woodpecker are often seen in the wood, along with good numbers of treecreepers and nuthatches. As **roe deer** often come into the wood to feed, fenced areas have been created to protect the young trees. Bastow Wood is a good area for **butterflies**, with small copper, small blue and peacock frequent. In autumn Grass Wood is a superb place for **fungi**, with many uncommon species.

Walk 5

Buckden

A scenic walk starting on the cobbled route of an old Roman road and leading up to magnificent views down the glaciated valley of the River Wharfe. After descending past the ancient church at Hubberholme, you return to Buckden via riverside meadows with spectacular displays of bistort. This is a walk to enjoy when fine weather allows you to appreciate the distant views down the valley.

FACTFILE

Distance: 5 miles (8 km)

Time needed: 3 hours

Starting point: SD 943774

Parking: Yorkshire Dales National Park car park, Buckden (£)

Paths: some uneven stretches, mixture of unsurfaced and surfaced (including some road)

Gradients: gentle-moderate

Refreshments: shop at Buckden; pubs there and in Hubberholme and Cray

Toilets: in car park

Public transport: daily bus service between Ilkley and Buckden (and on to Leeds and Bradford) during the summer

blue *best flower months*
pink *good flower months*

J F M A M J J A S O N D

FROM THE National Park car park at Bucken, follow the wide track through the gate and up towards Rakes Wood. This route is a rare remaining section of an old Roman road that was built to connect Ilkley to Bainbridge. It climbs steadily through Rakes Wood and then follows the contours of the hill along Buckden Rake.

The very first stretch is grazed and there are few flowers, although in spring and early summer the numerous **hawthorn** trees have a fine display of white blossom. The hillsides soon steepen and the scree slopes on the right are an excellent place to look for a range of limestone-loving flowers [1]. Most easy to spot are **wild thyme**, **eyebright**, **common rock-rose**, **mouse-ear hawkweed** and **selfheal**. Others include **creeping cinquefoil**, **hoary plantain**, **salad burnet** and the low-growing **carline thistle**. Search closely in late summer for the pinky-purple upright flowers of **autumn gentian**, also known as fell-wort.

Towards the end of the track, where the surface becomes more cobbled, there are some rocky limestone outcrops. Similar species occur here as on the scree slopes, but a careful search reveals the tiny **thyme-**

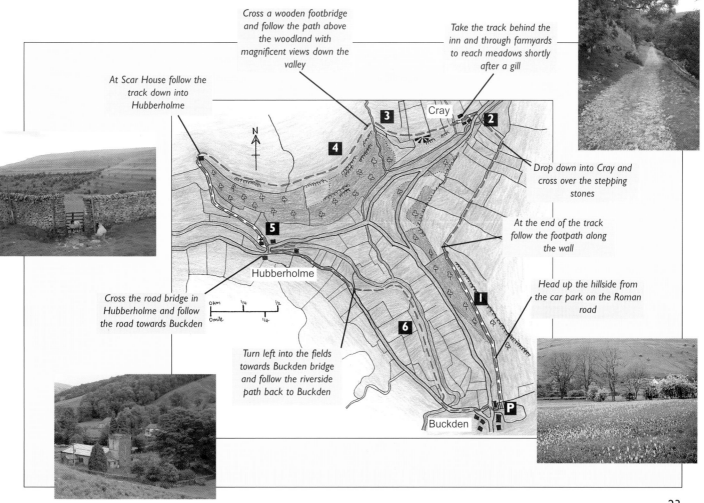

Cross a wooden footbridge and follow the path above the woodland with magnificent views down the valley

Take the track behind the inn and through farmyards to reach meadows shortly after a gill

At Scar House follow the track down into Hubberholme

Cray

3

2

4

Drop down into Cray and cross over the stepping stones

5

At the end of the track follow the footpath along the wall

Hubberholme

Head up the hillside from the car park on the Roman road

Cross the road bridge in Hubberholme and follow the road towards Buckden

0km   1/4   1/2
0mile   1/4

1

6

Turn left into the fields towards Buckden bridge and follow the riverside path back to Buckden

P

Buckden

-leaved sandwort, **fairy flax, parsley-piert** and **limestone bedstraw. Blue moor-grass, wild strawberry, black medick** and **wall-rue** are also found here.

At the end of the track follow the footpath along the wall to the left. Through the gate the fields are grazed and improved with few wildflowers. Keep an eye out for birds like wheatear and redstart perching on the stone walls. The footpath continues on the level, following the stone wall along the contour of the hill. After you have passed through a stile look out for a small path on the left which takes you down the steep hillside into the hamlet of Cray.

Before you cross the stepping stones over Cray Gill [2], look among the taller streamside vegetation for **meadowsweet, tufted vetch, meadow crane's-bill, common knapweed** and **colt's-foot.** Over the road, take the track behind the inn and through the farmyards. **Giant bellflower, shining crane's-bill, hedge woundwort** and **cut-leaved crane's-bill** grow at the base of the dry stone walls here.

Shortly the track fords a gill where you can find **yellow rattle, red bartsia, ragged-robin, water mint, brooklime, marsh-marigold** and **water-cress.** Follow the path signed 'Scar House and Yockenthwaite' which leads you through a number of hay meadows. The meadows can be colour-washed with the purple-tinge of the grass **Yorkshire fog** and the deeper red of **common sorrel. Meadow crane's-bill** and **crosswort** form brighter points of blue and yellow.

The path dips down to a wooden footbridge over Crook Gill [3]. Just before this is a meadow bank covered in **betony, field scabious, burnet-saxifrage, pignut, harebell, great burnet** and more unusually **kidney vetch.** Other lime-loving species seen before, including **common rock-rose,** also grow here.

After the footbridge continue through the well-grazed pasture land. On your left, over the tree tops, are magnificent views across the head of Wharfedale, clearly showing the glaciated U-shaped valley. The **ash** woodland on the hillside and the small patches of limestone pavement at your feet have been fenced to restrict grazing and allow regeneration of trees and wildflowers [4]. Look out for the blossom of **hawthorn** and cherry trees among the **ash** and **sycamore** trees, and for typical limestone flowers in the grikes between the pavement blocks.

Eventually you reach Scar House (dated 1676) where you follow the sign to Hubberholme round between the house and its barns. Continue down the concrete track to the low, solid Hubberholme church. This was once a forest chapel and the church is worth a look inside if you have the time. It retains a painted oak rood-loft where musicians once played, which dates back to the 16th century and is one of only two remaining in Yorkshire churches. The oak pews bear the trademark carved mouse of Thompson of Kilburn. Interpretative information is available within the church to guide you around the other interesting features.

At Hubberholme, pass the church and bear right onto the road, crossing the bridge over the River Wharfe [5]. The damp conditions on the riverbank support the giant leaves of butterbur, so-called because the large cool leaves were once used for wrapping butter. **Yellow iris** is also found here, its large bright flower a striking sight in late spring. This garden favourite is mainly pollinated by bees, which climb inside the flowers to reach the nectar.

From the bridge turn left onto Dubb's Lane in the direction of Buckden. After a short distance follow the footpath on the left signed 'Buckden Bridge' through a gate into the riverside meadows [6]. In May large patches of **common bistort** cover these damp meadows in stunning displays, their pale pink flower spikes spreading as far as the eye can see. The young leaves of this striking plant are used to make Easter-ledge, a traditional pudding. The snake-like shape of the plant's underground stems has given rise to the local name 'snakewort'. Both **wood crane's-bill** and **meadow crane's-bill** grow alongside the bistort in the meadow, with other species including **meadow vetchling**, **yellow rattle**, **great burnet**, **melancholy thistle** and **goat's-beard**. The alternative name for the goat's-beard, 'Jack-go-to-bed-at-noon', refers to the fact that the flower closes up during the heat of the day, only to appear again at dawn.

Follow the riverside path to Buckden Bridge where you rejoin the road and cross back over the River Wharfe via a sturdy stone bridge. Look here for dipper and grey wagtail on the river, then walk back up into Buckden village where your walk began. ✿

Other wildlife

The woods along this walk are frequented by a variety of **birds**, such as goldcrest, green woodpecker and redstart. In the valley there are oystercatchers and curlews, along with many wheatears. **Hares** are sometimes seen in the area.

Walk 6 — Langstrothdale

A gentle riverside walk which takes you through the isolated upper valley of the River Wharfe. The fast river often tumbles over small falls and rocky outcrops, but in dry summers it is known to disappear as the water sinks into the fissured limestone. Lime-rich springs gush out from the open hillside, and clusters of stout barns mark the traditional walled hay meadows.

FACTFILE

Distance: 4.6 mi (7.4 km)

Time needed: 3 hours

Starting point: SD 904791

Parking: by roadside between Yockenthwaite and Deepdale

Paths: even, mixture of unsurfaced and surfaced (including some road)

Gradients: gentle

Refreshments: nearest in Buckden

Toilets: nearest public toilets Buckden

Public transport: nearest bus stop Buckden

blue *best flower months*
pink *good flower months*

J F M A M J J A S O N D

THE WALK starts along the open road from Yockenthwaite to Deepdale. Springs along the hillside create a series of wet flushes which support a wide variety of flowers [1]. The small pink flowers of **bird's-eye primrose** are common. Look closely to see the yellow eye at the centre of the petals, and at the small rosette of leaves that are mealy-white below. Also present here are **common butterwort**, **tormentil**, **marsh valerian**, **salad burnet**, **common milkwort**, **common bird's-foot trefoil**, **mouse-ear hawkweed**, **hoary plantain** and **cuckooflower**. A variety of grasses and sedges are well represented too, including the lime-loving **blue moor-grass**, the delicate **quaking grass** and the familiar white tops of **common cottongrass**. Mounds of the pale green *Sphagnum* moss grow in places. Even the tiny roadside drain has interest with **brooklime**, **lesser spearwort** and the greeny-white flowers of the more unusual **grass-of-parnassus**.

Further along the road is a small rocky outcrop which brings some of these small plants nearer to eye-level [2]. A closer look at the waxy leaves of **common butterwort** reveals the small insects trapped by the

Bird's eye primrose

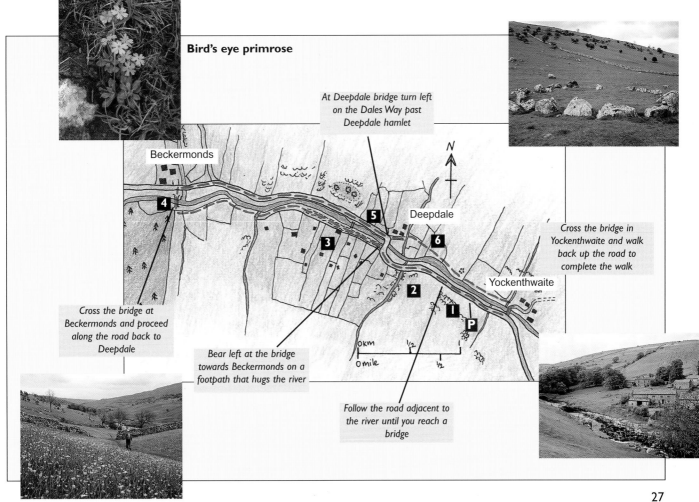

Beckermonds

At Deepdale bridge turn left on the Dales Way past Deepdale hamlet

Deepdale

N

Cross the bridge in Yockenthwaite and walk back up the road to complete the walk

Yockenthwaite

Cross the bridge at Beckermonds and proceed along the road back to Deepdale

Bear left at the bridge towards Beckermonds on a footpath that hugs the river

Follow the road adjacent to the river until you reach a bridge

0km   ½   1
0mile   ½

plant to provide it with extra nutrients. You can more easily see the delicate purple-blue on the small flower heads of the **blue moor-grass**. Other flowers here include **fairy flax, harebell, wild thyme, limestone bedstraw, burnet-saxifrage** and violets. The ferns **green spleenwort** and **wall-rue** are tucked into the cracks in the rock.

Hagg Gill joins the road at a small gorge where you will find **primrose, crosswort, lady's-mantle** and **sweet cicely**. The river banks support **silverweed, lady's bedstraw, pignut** and **butterbur**.

Carry on along the road to Deepdale Bridge and follow the footpath on the left of the river, signed 'Beckermonds' and the 'Dales Way'. The river bank has patches of **colt's-foot** and **common knapweed**. In damper areas **common scurvygrass, monkeyflower, bay willow** and **meadowsweet** grow.

Shortly you will see clusters of barns in the smaller walled fields on your left [3]. These barns have traditionally stored hay from the flower-rich meadows and provided shelter for farm animals over the winter. There is no access into the meadows, but if you look over the walls and through gateways you will be rewarded by the colourful sight of a range of wildflowers. Look out for **red clover, meadow buttercup, melancholy thistle, great burnet, eyebright, yellow rattle, bugle, meadow crane's-bill, cow parsley** and **germander speedwell**.

The path continues on past a footbridge and a house, following the line of the River Wharfe all the way to Beckermonds. Keep an eye out for riverside plants like **monkeyflower, large bitter-cress, water mint** and **marsh-marigold**. If you are lucky a kingfisher will flash by here, its electric-blue plumage making a vivid display.

At Beckermonds cross the footbridge into the hamlet [4]. A quick search along the shady roadside walls reveals **shining crane's-bill, rue-leaved saxifrage** and **common whitlowgrass** among the escaped garden plants and stonecrops. Follow the road across the River Wharfe and turn right at the junction towards Buckden. The roadside

verge here has little wildflower interest; being nutrient rich it has large stands of nettle and thistles, and patches of the invasive **bracken**. There are, however, fantastic displays of **hawthorn** or May blossom on the hill slopes above the road in early summer. The white flowers of this low tree are striking.

Just before Deepdale [5] look out for more riverside flushes with the species mentioned earlier, plus **watercress, water avens, common milkwort** and **hedge woundwort**. The name 'woundwort' refers to the medicinal use of the plant to stem bleeding. The plant's green parts were made into a poultice and applied to the wound. Modern studies have shown that oil contained in woundwort does indeed have antiseptic properties. At Deepdale Bridge turn left toward the hamlet of Deepdale along the Dales Way. The footpath bears right through a gate and down to a footbridge over Deepdale Gill where the banksides are covered in swathes of **ramsons**. It then bears left up the slope and follows the wall to a stile and a lichen-encrusted footpath sign.

Over the stile [6] you enter National Trust property and meadows, yellow with **meadow buttercup, yellow rattle** and **crosswort**. There is also an abundance of **pignut, red clover, common mouse-ear, cow parsley, common sorrel, yarrow, eyebright** and **germander speedwell**. The field edges have odd remnants of woodland flora including **dog's mercury** and **bluebell**.

The path joins the riverside and as you step over the stile at the wall you enter an open field of improved grassland where wildflowers are scarce. Look out instead for the small Bronze Age circle of stones which dates back to 2000 BC. No-one can be sure why it is situated here but one opinion holds it to be a burial site. As you approach Yockenthwaite there is a more recent historical structure, a limekiln built into the slope and used in the 18th and 19th centuries for converting limestone into lime. The lime was used to spread on acid soil to improve fertility. Now the kiln is crumbling and **maidenhair spleenwort** grows in its crevaces.

Go through the gate into Yockenthwaite and right over the beautiful, arching stone bridge. More **maidenhair spleenwort** and **wall-rue** can be seen on its walled sides. You are now back at the open road at the start of the walk. ✿

Other wildlife

There are several **birds** to look for along the river, including common sandpiper, grey wagtail, dipper and oystercatcher. Buzzards are sometimes seen in this part of Wharfedale, along with twite, a montane cousin of the linnet. In the riverside trees there are frequently flocks of redpoll and siskin, and along the dry stone walls wheatears are often present.

Walk 7 — Skipton Wood

An easy stroll around this Woodland Trust reserve, famous for its stunning spring displays of bluebells and ramsoms, but also supporting a range of other interesting flowers. The walk takes you along part of a heritage trail past the ramparts of the imposing Skipton Castle, perched impressively on top of a cliff above the stream known as Eller Beck.

FACTFILE

Distance: 2.4 mi (3.8 km)

Time needed: 2 hours

Starting point: SD 992518

Parking: car park at north end of Skipton High St, (£)

Paths: mostly even, some surfaced (including some road and pavement), others can be muddy

Gradients: gentle-moderate, a few steep steps

Refreshments: wide variety in Skipton

Toilets: in car park

Public transport: Skipton has a railway and bus station

blue *best flower months*
pink *good flower months*

J F M A M J J A S O N D

PARK IN the main car park in Skipton (pay and display) and walk in the direction of the castle. Cross over the busy road at the roundabout and join the B6265 Grassington road. Shortly after crossing the canal, some steps lead down to a small garden and on to a footpath past some mill buildings, one with an ageing water wheel still in place.

Soon you enter an open area where the footpath is raised up from water on both sides [1]. To the left is Eller Beck, the source of power for the mills on which much of Skipton's wealth was built. On the right-hand side runs an arm of the Leeds-Liverpool canal system, now taking mainly pleasure craft, but in times of old a major transport artery. This first section of the walk follows a heritage trail marked by metal plaques. Along this stretch look for **wood avens**, **feverfew**, **water forget-me-not**, **dog's mercury**, **garlic mustard**, **hedge woundwort** and **hart's tongue** at the edge of the path. There are many trees bordering the river here, including **hornbeam**, several **wych elms** and the smaller **elder**, with its pretty white blossoms.

A little further on the impressive sight

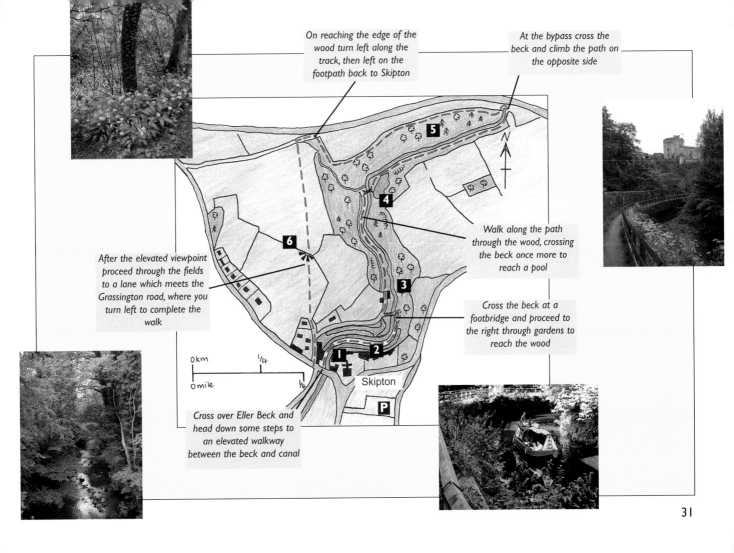

On reaching the edge of the wood turn left along the track, then left on the footpath back to Skipton

At the bypass cross the beck and climb the path on the opposite side

Walk along the path through the wood, crossing the beck once more to reach a pool

After the elevated viewpoint proceed through the fields to a lane which meets the Grassington road, where you turn left to complete the walk

Cross the beck at a footbridge and proceed to the right through gardens to reach the wood

Skipton

0 km · 1/4 · 1/2

0 mile · 1/4

Cross over Eller Beck and head down some steps to an elevated walkway between the beck and canal of Skipton Castle comes into view to your right [2]. It occupies an impregnable position at the top of an stone steep river cliff, which no doubt contributed to its long unconquered history. Look out for curtains of **ivy** on the rock face here, and a variety of ferns which like the humid, shady conditions in the long shadow of the castle.

Continue until you reach a footbridge over the river, cross this and take a track to the right, which leads somewhat unexpectedly through a private garden before you enter Skipton Wood Woodland Trust reserve via a gate [3]. The signboard gives further information about the trust and the wood, which supports 17 types

of tree, over 160 types of wild flower, and is thought to date back over 1,000 years. Common tree species in the wood are **beech**, **ash** and **sycamore**, but with so many other tree species on offer, the wood is an excellent place to practise your tree identification skills.

An early spring visit is highly recommended, as the wood contains some of the Dales' finest displays of **bluebells** and **ramsons**. At the peak time (usually May) the air is heady with the strong odour of the **ramsons**, a herb which was used extensively for culinary purposes in the past. Sharing the soil with these high profile species is a range of other interesting woodland flowers. They include **enchanter's-nightshade**, **red campion**, **water avens**, **greater burdock** and **opposite-leaved golden-saxifrage**. There are several scarce species to look for, notably **herb-paris** and **goldilocks buttercup**, which can be difficult to locate.

The woodland track is well defined and leads over another footbridge over the beck to a pond where kingfishers sometimes hunt [4]. At the margins look for **large bitter-cress**, **butterbur** and **wild angelica**. Shortly after the pond the track forks; take the left-hand fork which passes through an area of damp grassland in a clearing by the beck, where **meadowsweet** and **branched bur-reed** grow. A little further on look for the distinctive **lords-and-ladies** under the trees. This unusual plant has glossy, arrow-shaped leaves; a bizarre sheath grows up later in the year enclosing a purple organ known as the spadix. This feature gives rise to the plant's other name, preacher-in-the-pulpit. In summer the plant produces a mass of poisonous orange berries which cling to the stem. Also in this area are **wood anemone, wood-sorrel** and **brooklime**.

Soon you will reach the Skipton by-pass where you must once again cross a footbridge over the beck, this time part of the by-pass construction itself. From here the path climbs into a section of the wood with a different character, where **sweet chestnut, holly** and **yew** trees grow alongside conifers [5]. For centuries local people have relied on the wood for food, fuel and building materials and the sweet chestnut and conifers were probably planted for commercial reasons. This is a good place to look for the elusive **goldilocks buttercup**. It is a smaller member of the buttercup family, with golden-yellow petals and distinctive kidney-shaped root leaves. The goldilocks buttercup likes basic or neutral soils, and occurs only at a small number of other sites in the southern Dales.

Continue on the track until you reach the edge of the wood, looking out for a fascinating array of animal tracks carved into a wooden bench part way along this section. Once outside the wood follow the footpath signed 'Skipton High Street' which leads up through open fields to a superb viewpoint over the town at Park Hill [6]. As you study the geography of the town, consider the people who stood on this spot centuries before you, looking down the Aire valley for hostile invaders from the south.

The path continues on past fields outlined by **hawthorn** hedges, which in May are lit up with white blossom, giving rise to another of its names, May blossom. These quick-growing trees have been used for centuries as field boundaries. They are excellent nesting sites for birds and later in the year yield a berry crop which is an important winter food source for thrushes. Soon you reach the lane which takes you back down to Grassington Road past some pretty cottages. When you reach the road, turn left and you will be back where you started the walk. From here it is a short stroll back to the car park. ✿

Other wildlife

The wood is an excellent site for **birds**, with numerous different warbler species, plus goldcrest, spotted flycatcher, great-spotted and green woodpeckers and sparrowhawk. Around the pond look for grey heron, grey wagtail and kingfisher. Among the **mammals**, roe deer frequently visit the wood, which supports an impressive five species of bats. In the stream look for the native **white-clawed crayfish**, which is slowly being displaced in the Dales by more aggressive introduced species.

Walk 8 — *Malham Tarn*

This short walk amid dramatic limestone scenery takes you through a superb fen, woodland and damp grassland, which together support a stunning array of plant species. The whole area is internationally important for its wildlife, and a walk in June or July will be rewarded by opportunities to see the many unusual plants adapted to the damp conditions.

FACTFILE

Distance: 3.7 mi (6 km)

Time needed: 3 hours

Starting point: SD 894657

Parking: in rough parking area just off minor road south of tarn

Paths: even, mostly surfaced (including some boardwalk and road)

Gradients: gentle

Refreshments: Ice Cream van in summer in car parking area, otherwise pub and shop in Malham village (3 mi to south)

Toilets: Malham village

Public transport: weekend and bank holiday bus service between Leeds, Bradford, Skipton and Malham

Notes: a permit *must* be obtained to enter the fen from the FSC office (01729 830331)
blue *best flower months*
pink *good flower months*

J F M A M J J A S O N D

THE WALK starts from the small (sometimes muddy) car parking area a short distance south of Malham Tarn. Taking the left-hand grassy path, you pass through a section of rather grazed acid grassland [1]. In this area **tormentil, heath bedstraw, wild thyme, heath speedwell** and **selfheal** are common, together with a few patches of **bilberry, heather** and **lady's bedstraw**. The grasses, rushes and sedges which grow here, including **mat-grass** and **heath rush**, are hardy species tolerant of grazing and are adapted to the acidic soil conditions. In a few places the ground is boggy and here impressive stands of **common cottongrass** grow, together with the beautiful **bog asphodel, cuckooflower, lesser spearwort** and **marsh-marigold**.

Pause where the small outflow stream leaves the tarn and admire the view across one of Yorkshire's few natural lakes. It is the only upland alkaline lake in the UK and one of only eight in Europe. This is a good place to look for plants which like the wet conditions at the stream edges, such as **meadowsweet** and **water mint**.

Soon you reach a walled plantation at the tarn's edge, and a short distance afterwards

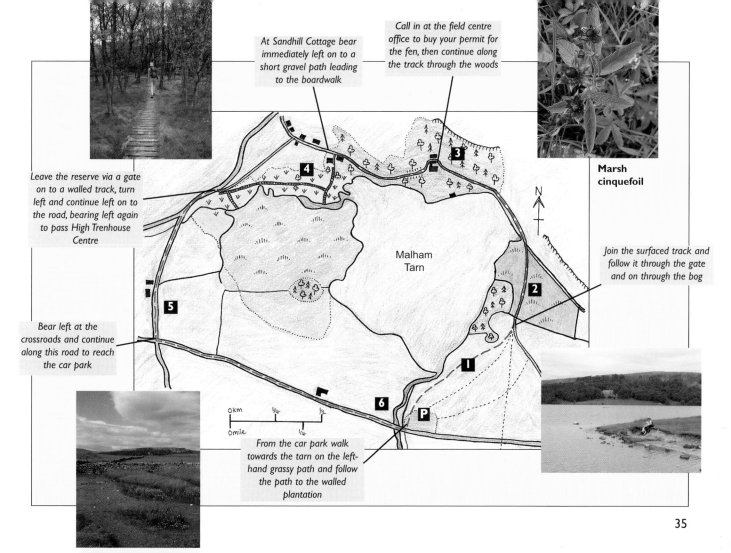

At Sandhill Cottage bear immediately left on to a short gravel path leading to the boardwalk

Call in at the field centre office to buy your permit for the fen, then continue along the track through the woods

Marsh cinquefoil

Leave the reserve via a gate on to a walled track, turn left and continue left on to the road, bearing left again to pass High Trenhouse Centre

Join the surfaced track and follow it through the gate and on through the bog

Bear left at the crossroads and continue along this road to reach the car park

Malham Tarn

N

From the car park walk towards the tarn on the left-hand grassy path and follow the path to the walled plantation

0km   ¼   ½
0mile   ¼

4
3
5
2
1
6
P

join a surfaced track which leads to a gate onto a peat bog [2]. This area is very diverse in plant life compared with the acid grassland you have just walked through. Look out for the delicate **bird's-eye primrose**, plus **common butterwort**, **devils'-bit scabious**, **marsh lousewort**, **marsh valerian** and **common milkwort**. Areas of **quaking grass** occur here, the neat compact flower heads nodding in the breeze. Where streams run across the bog **water-cress**, **brooklime** and a variety of lime-loving sedges grow.

Continue on from the bog along the track and you will shortly reach the woodland on the northern edge of the tarn [3]. This largely planted woodland supports a variety of tree species, including **ash**, **sycamore**, **rowan**, **European larch** and **yew**. The ground flora includes **dog's mercury**, **herb-robert**, **hedge woundwort** and **enchanter's nightshade**. Look out for both **wood avens** and **water avens**, together with their hybrid form. Various species such as monk's-hood and fairy foxglove have escaped from the gardens of Tarn House.

A permit is needed to walk through the unusual fen and carr on the far side of the Tarn. This can be purchased for £1 from the Field Studies Council office at Tarn House, just inside the main entrance which faces your approach. The prominent Victorian politician Walter Morrison was a previous owner of the house, and spent many summers here in the company of visitors such as Charles Kingsley and John Ruskin. He was remembered as a generous landlord, often donating time and money to the local community.

After buying your permit, continue on the track around the back of the house and on between high walls of a cutting, where you will find more woodland flowers like **ramsons** and various ferns. A little further along is a path to a bird hide at the Tarn's edge. From here you may see coots and great crested grebes on the water, and curlews on the muddy margins.

At Sandhill Cottage turn left from the track, keeping the cottage on your right. A short gravel path soon leads

to a wooden boardwalk taking you under lichen-covered willow carr [4]. **Marsh-marigold, ragged robin, bogbean, marsh cinquefoil** and **wild angelica** all thrive in the damp conditions and hummocks of *Sphagnum* moss form pale green patches. The boardwalk continues onto some higher ground where the acid peat supports **purple moor-grass, bilberry, heather** and **wavy hair-grass**. Look out for bog plants such as the insectivorous **round-leaved sundew, bog asphodel, deergrass** and if you are lucky, the rare **bog-rosemary**. The last section of boardwalk passes over a very diverse fen with numerous lemon-flowered **globeflower**, plus **melancholy thistle, marsh hawk's-beard, marsh lousewort, great burnet, saw-wort** and **yellow rattle**. This latter species has declined recently as hay meadows have been 'improved' through re-seeding and by the addition of fertilizer. Its name refers to the seeds which rattle around inside the capsule.

Leave the reserve via the gate onto a walled track and bear left onto the road. Continue on the road in the direction of Malham village, turning left at both of the two road junctions. The contrast between the nature reserve and the species-poor grazed fields is remarkable, but there are still various road-side flowers to see [5]. You can find **sweet cicely, bush vetch, lady's bedstraw, germander speedwell, crosswort, common bird's-foot-trefoil, pignut** and **yarrow**. Enjoy the good views across Tarn Moss to the wooded Spiggot Hill, and look out on your right for the tall smelt-mill chimney which was used to melt lead mined on Malham Moor. Curlews nest in the surrounding fields, their evocative calls ringing out over the fells in spring. Other wading birds such as oystercatcher and redshank are sometimes also seen in this area.

Eventually the road brings you back to the Tarn outflow stream [6] and the car park. The stream continues to the south for a short distance, then sinks into the limestone. Take time before leaving to explore the stream sides where marsh-orchids, **water-cress, water forget-me-not, water mint, marsh-marigold, cuckooflower** and **common marsh-bedstraw** grow. ✹

Other wildlife

The tarn is an good place for **birds**, with nesting coot, great-crested grebe and mallard. In winter large flocks of other duck gather on the water. Dipper and grey wagtail frequent the streams and curlew are often seen at the water's edge. There are often birds of prey on the wing, including kestrel, sparrowhawk, peregrine and merlin. The woods support a variety of woodland birds such as nuthatch and commoner warblers. **Mammals** include both Daubenton's and pipistrelle bats, fox and roe deer. There are many types of fish in the tarn, including bullhead, brown trout, perch and stone loach. There are **butterflies** such as peacock, small blue and small heath and many **dragonflies** and **damselflies** frequent the small pools on the bog.

Walk 9   *Langcliffe Scars*

This bracing walk winds along a flower-filled green lane, before climbing up to cross the Plantlife reserve at Winskill Stones, which protects precious fragments of limestone pavement. It provides opportunities to see some specialised plants adapted to the conditions on the pavement, as well as a range of interesting and uncommon species in the surrounding pasture and meadows.

FACTFILE

Distance: 3.2 mi (5.1 km)

Time needed: 3 hours

Starting point: SD 824651

Parking: by Langcliffe school

Paths: mainly even grassy paths, with some road

Gradients: moderate-steep

Refreshments: wide variety in Settle (1 mi to south)

Toilets: Settle

Public transport: regular bus service between Skipton and Settle; railway station in Settle on main line from Leeds to Carlisle

blue *best flower months*
pink *good flower months*

J	F	M	A	M	J	J	A	S	O	N	D

PARK BY the village school and proceed to the left along a lane. Take a right-hand fork to reach a walled green lane which heads out of the village. This lane has a profusion of wild flowers growing at its edges and on the walls [1]. Look out for **shining crane's-bill**, **ivy-leaved toadflax**, **crosswort**, **oxeye daisy**, **meadow crane's-bill**, **bush vetch**, **hedge woundwort**, **field scabious**, **wood avens**, **meadowsweet** and **lady's bedstraw**. Soon the impressive sight of Stainforth Scar, a former quarry, comes into view, with Ingleborough beyond it.

The green lane ends at a gate. Go through this and join a path that leads you up to the right-hand side of Stainforth Scar through fields with a range of flowers [2]. Look out for **betony**, **wild strawberry**, **germander speedwell**, **eyebright**, **wild thyme**, **salad burnet**, **mouse-ear hawkweed** and **common bird's-foot-trefoil**.

When level with the top of the scar proceed through a stile and upwards on a path through walled fields. On reaching a minor road bear right and continue for a short stretch, looking out for limestone outcrops by the roadside with **common rock-rose**, **fairy flax**, **hoary plantain** and

On reaching a track bear right, and at the road right again towards a cutting

After the cutting proceed down the road towards Langcliffe

Bear right, staying on the main road which brings you back to Langcliffe

Shining crane's-bill

Shortly after the farm buildings head due east to cross scattered limestone pavement

Common rock-rose

Proceed on through walled fields to reach a minor road and bear right

N

Langcliffe

At the end of the green lane continue through the gate on a footpath which climbs up towards woodland

Take the lane left of the school which leads to a green lane heading out of the village

0 km   1/4   1/2
0 mile   1/4

1 **2** **3** **4** **5** **6** **P**

quaking grass [3]. Immediately after joining the road bear left, not on the the wall-side track signed 'Catrigg Force', but due east across the scattered limestone pavement on a poorly-defined path. As you wander among the scattered limestone pavements keep a look out for plants nestling among them, such as **limestone bedstraw**, **mountain pansy**, **dog's mercury** and ferns including **hart's tongue**, **maidenhair spleenwort** and **wall-rue** [4]. In spring this is an excellent area for **early-purple orchid**, the strongly spotted leaves revealing their presence long after the purple flower spikes have withered.

Proceed through a stone stile in the dry stone wall and you soon reach a track. Bear right here and you will shortly meet the B6479 that joins Langcliffe with Malham. Here you enter for the first time the Plantlife reserve of Winskill Stones, which protects fragments of limestone pavement, one of Britain's most threatened habitats. The pavements have been formed from the combined action of glaciers, which stripped the soil around 10,000 years ago, and more recent erosion by the elements. Blocks (clints) and fissures (grikes) characterise the pavement landscape. It is a harsh environment, with strong winds and wide variations in temperature and moisture levels. Many plants enjoy the conditions in the grikes, where there is soil and protection from the wind. The area was saved in 1996 from total destruction for use in garden rockeries, when Plantlife raised the money to buy it through a campaign led by the late Geoff Hamilton. Light grazing is used during summer and autumn to maintain the botanical interest of the site. Animals are excluded during the winter and in spring to allow wild flowers to become established.

Continue down the road and into a gorge-like cutting with much botanical interest on the limestone crags and sheltered grassland below [5]. Plantlife have an open access policy on the reserve, allowing you to explore away from the road. However, beware of the slippery rocks and hidden hollows between the limestone blocks, which have broken many walkers' ankles in the Dales. Look among the rocks for **wall lettuce**, **wild thyme**, **blue moor-grass** and **hairy rock-cress**, plus a range of ferns including the more unusual **green spleenwort**, **rigid buckler-fern** and **brittle bladder-fern**. The limestone sward here is very rich, supporting species such as **carline thistle**, **eyebright**, **field scabious**, **mountain pansy**, **cuckoo-flower**, **burnet-saxifrage** and **heath speedwell**. In order to appreciate the full range of species, it is necessary to get down on your knees here!

A little gem to look for here is the very local **mountain everlasting**. This small plant grows in only a few places in the Dales, chiefly in dry limestone pastures in upland areas. The woody flowering stems bear tiny white flowers in June and July, with the male and female plants having a completely different appearance. Whereas the male flowers are typical open flower heads consisting of florets ringed by bracts, the female plants have a cluster of flower heads at the end of the stem, each with long woolly bracts that enclose the florets. After seeding the flowers drop off to reveal the seeds with their white parachutes of hairs. The 'everlasting' label may have two origins; first the perennial nature of the plant, appearing in the same spot year after year, and second its use for winter decoration as a dried plant in times of old. Its other name, cat's foot, refers to the soft feel and appearance of the plant.

Proceed down the quiet road in the direction of Langcliffe, pausing to investigate the well-preserved lime kiln dotted with ferns. Such lime kilns were once a common feature in the Dales, used to produce a powder that reduced the acidity of pastures. Carry on past a car parking area on your left, with an information board about the reserve. As you walk down the road enjoy the splendid view across the valley below you [6]. This is another good area for **early purple-orchid** and **mountain pansy**.

Follow the road as it winds down steeply into Langcliffe, looking out for flowers on the roadside and in the fields either side. Here **common milkwort** and **common spotted-orchid** grow in addition to the species already mentioned. As you near the outskirts of Langcliffe, you will see the twiggy nests of rooks in the tall trees in the churchyard. Continue past the church and on to the school where your walk began. ✿

Other wildlife

There are quite a few **birds** to look for along this walk, including several types of finch, peregrine falcon, raven and wheatear. There is a rookery in the churchyard. Among the many rabbits look for **hares**, larger and with longer legs and black tips to the ears. The sunny slopes are good for **butterflies**, with small blue, small copper and small skipper likely.

Walk 10

Ingleborough

This strenuous walk on the lower slopes of Ingleborough is not for the faint hearted. It crosses a wild landscape of rugged limestone pavements filled with exciting and unusual plants, before reaching the only juniper woodland in North Yorkshire. Those willing to take on the challenge will be rewarded by unforgettable views and a glimpse of what much of the region must have looked like at the end of the ice age.

FACTFILE

Distance: 5.5 mi (8.8 km)

Time needed: 4.5 hours

Starting point: SD 808726

Parking: in Yorkshire Dales National Park car park, Horton-in-Ribblesdale (£)

Paths: uneven and difficult in places, unsurfaced

Gradients: moderate-steep

Refreshments: cafe and shop in Horton-in-Ribblesdale

Toilets: Horton-in-Ribblesdale, in car park

Public transport: limited bus service between Settle and Horton-in-Ribblesdale; train station in Horton-in-Ribblesdale on Leeds-Carlisle route

blue *best flower months*
pink *good flower months*

J F M A M J J A S O N D

FROM THE car park in the pretty village of Horton-in-Ribblesdale, follow the track past the toilet block and cross over the river Ribble via an impressive wooden footbridge. You will see the sphinx-like profile of Pen-y-ghent, the smallest of the famous Three Peaks, dominating the village to the east. Turn your back on this peak and walk to your left along the road, in the direction of Ingleborough. At the railway station, cross the line, taking care to look for trains passing on the busy Settle-Carlisle route.

The first section of the walk climbs through rather poor, well-grazed grassland with few wild flowers [1]. The main compensation here is the fine view across the Ribble valley back towards Pen-y-ghent. After the third stile you reach the boundary sign for Ingleborough National Nature Reserve, and immediately enter an interesting area of limestone grassland [2]. Among the short grasses grow **eyebright, fairy flax, harebell, wild thyme, quaking grass, common rock-rose, lady's bedstraw** and **mouse-ear hawkweed**. Look carefully for the beautiful **autumn gentian**, bearing in mind that its purple flowers are not usually seen until late July.

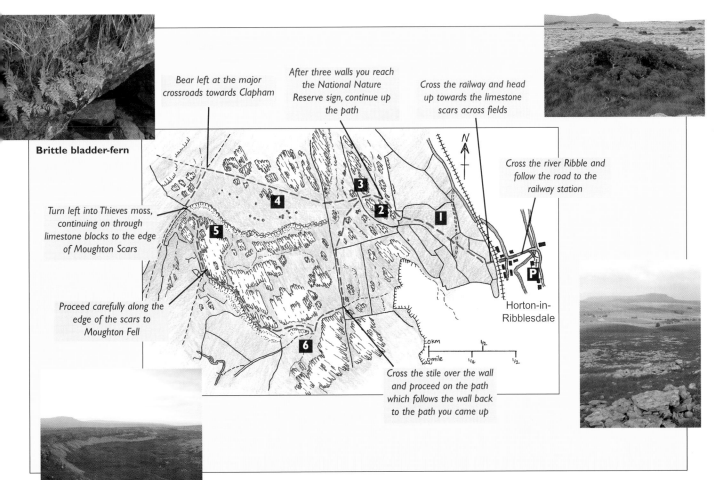

Brittle bladder-fern

Bear left at the major crossroads towards Clapham

After three walls you reach the National Nature Reserve sign, continue up the path

Cross the railway and head up towards the limestone scars across fields

Cross the river Ribble and follow the road to the railway station

Turn left into Thieves moss, continuing on through limestone blocks to the edge of Moughton Scars

Proceed carefully along the edge of the scars to Moughton Fell

Cross the stile over the wall and proceed on the path which follows the wall back to the path you came up

Horton-in-Ribblesdale

3
4
2
1
5
6
P

N

0km   1/4   1/2
0mile   1/2

Continuing on the path you reach the first outcrops of exposed limestone [3]. The gaps between the rocks are known as grikes and these provide the sheltered conditions favoured by a variety of plants that form magnificent natural rock gardens. They include **lesser meadow-rue**, **crosswort**, **wall lettuce** and many woodland species such as **herb-robert**, **dog's mercury**, **sanicle** and **wood sorrel**. Ferns enjoy the humid conditions in the grikes, with **hart's tongue**, **brittle bladder-fern**, **green spleenwort** and **wall-rue** all present. The green spleenwort is a local species occurring only on limestone rocks.

The track continues on towards the summit of Ingleborough and along this section you will probably see fell walkers on their way round the 25-mile Three Peaks circuit. At Sulber Nick [4] the path enters a peaty area where the ground is waterlogged. This raised bog is typified by **deergrass**, **mat-grass**, **heather**, **bilberry**, **lousewort**, **common cottongrass** and **bog asphodel**. There are several small pools and here *Sphagnum* moss grows in abundance, often with the insectivorous **round-leaved sundew**. If you look closely at the leaves of this remarkable little plant you will see tiny dew-like droplets; these are sticky and trap insects, making the sundew one of Britain's few native plant species to capture live prey. Its small white flowers are suspended on short stalks which raise the plant a few centimetres off the bog.

Common butterwort, another insectivorous species, grows only a short distance away. This violet-flowered gem grows in seepage areas near the crumbling limestone outcrops, and captures insects on its slimy leaves. It often grows in association with one of the Dales' finest flowers, the **bird's-eye primrose**. The outcrops themselves support a completely different flora to that found on the peat bog. Here, **blue moor-grass**, **carline thistle** and **lady's mantle** nestle among the rocks. Ingleborough is home to several different types of lady's mantle which are rather difficult to tell apart, including one minute species, *Alchemilla minima*, which grows no-where else in

the world but upper Ribblesdale. Along with the tiny, white-flowered **English sandwort**, which grows nearby, this makes Ingleborough one of the foremost sites in Britain for so-called endemic plant species.

On reaching the footpath sign bear left in the direction of Clapham away from the busy track. You will really feel you are in the uplands at this point, with panoramic views of the surrounding peaks and the nearby Moughton Fell, dotted with dark green patches of **juniper**. You will soon reach a wall with a large gate-way. Go through this gate, and turn immediately left through a small pedestrian gate. Below you is the ampitheatre which forms the head of Crummackdale [5]. It is a strange moonscape consisting of large expanses of limestone pavement, pocked with impressively deep grikes.

Walk down into the ampitheatre and as you cross the boggy Thieves Moss look out for a poorly-marked path bearing to the right at a small cairn. The path dips gently down on a grassy route between the limestone blocks and shortly reaches Beggar Stile. Don't go over the stile, but turn left 10 metres before it, up onto the tops of the limestone pavement. Follow the edge of Moughton Scars which drops away steeply to the right, taking great care on this uneven ground. This is how much of the Dales must have looked at the end of the ice age when huge glaciers retreated, scraping bare the rock. In a few places

odd-shaped rocks known as erratics are perched on the pavements, left by the ice. These are made up of a different rock to the underlying limestone and may have originated some distance away. Take time to look for the limestone flowers as you pick your way between the stones. Many ferns grow here, together with some woodland species which find the shady conditions in the grikes to their liking, such as **wood anemone**.

After passing a short stretch of wall and several stone-built grouse butts drop down and turn left onto a more well-trodden path. You are now at Moughton Fell itself with its stunted, weather-gnarled **juniper** trees [6] . If you crush the spiny leaves you can detect the distinctive smell of gin; the berries of this plant are used to make that popular drink.

Cross the stile on the long stone wall and follow its line to the left. The path descends the hillside and rejoins the one you came up. Retrace your steps to the railway station and onward to the car park. ✿

Other wildlife

Among the **birds**, keep an eye out for golden plover, merlin, peregrine falcon, raven, ring ousel and wheatear. There are several **butterflies** to see, including small heath. **Foxes** sometimes venture up to the pavements in search of prey.

Plant photographs

ON THE following pages there are photographs of over 80 different species of wild flowers, ferns and trees that you can see on the walks. This is only a selection of those species which are found in the Yorkshire Dales. We have included the more common species, and a few less common ones that are typical of the Yorkshire Dales.

Although this section is not intended to be an identification guide, we hope that the photographs will help those new to flowers to put a name to many of the species they will see on the walks. There is no substitute for a good identification guide and the further details of such guides are given on page 56.

The key explains the information given for each species illustrated. Their Latin names appear in the alphabetical listing on pages 58-60.

KEY TO PHOTOGRAPHS

Name - in English, following the Botanical Society of the British Isles publication *English names of wild flowers*

Height - of flowering stem in centimetres; for trees height in metres; for ferns leaf length in cm

Habitat - The range of habitats in which the species is found in the southern Yorkshire Dales. *Grassland* includes grazed pasture, tall meadows and roadsides. *Bogs* are acid wet areas, whereas *Fens* are alkaline wet areas

Flowering period - given as abbreviated months for flowers and trees; these are the main flowering months and plants can flower outside this period; plants growing at higher altitudes, or in shady crevaces, usually flower later in the year

Bog asphodel
10-30 cm; acid moors, bogs
Jul-Aug

Cowslip
15-30 cm; grassland, woods
Apr-May

Yellow-rattle
15-30 cm; grassland
May-Aug

Kidney vetch
15-25 cm; limestone grassland
Jun-Sep

Mountain pansy
5-10 cm; grassland
May-Aug

Carline thistle
10-25 cm; limestone grassland
Jul-Sep

Primrose
5-15 cm; grassland, woods
May-Jun

Common rock-rose
5-20 cm; limestone grassland, rocks
May-Sep

Biting stonecrop
2-8 cm; limestone rocks
Jun-Jul

Marsh hawk's-beard
30-90 cm; damp grassland, woods
Jul-Sep

Yellow flowers

Lady's bedstraw
15-35 cm; grassland
Apr-May

Common cow-wheat
10-40 cm; woods
May-Sep

Crosswort
15-30 cm; grassland, woods
May-Aug

Tormentil
5-10 cm; acid grassland, moors
Jun-Sep

Water avens
25-40 cm; damp grassland,
woods
May-Jul

Marsh-marigold
20-40 cm; wet places
Apr-May

Yellow iris
40-120 cm; wet places
May-Jul

Mouse-ear hawkweed
5-20 cm; grassland, rocks
May-Jul

Common ragwort
12-80 cm; grassland
Jun-Sep

Betony
10-40 cm; grassland
Jun-Sep

Bird's-eye primrose
5-20 cm; damp limestone
grassland
May-Jun

Common bistort
30-100 cm; damp grassland
Jun-Aug

Common spotted-orchid
15-40 cm; grassland, woods
Jun-Aug

Early-purple orchid
20-35 cm; limestone grassland,
woods
Mar-Jun

Lousewort
5-15 cm; damp acid grassland
Apr-Jul

Creeping thistle
30-80 cm; grassland
Jun-Sep

Melancholy thistle
45-100 cm; grassland
Jul-Aug

Saw-wort
25-50 cm; limestone grassland,
fens
Jul-Sep

Greater knapweed
15-50 cm; grassland
Jul-Sep

Pink or purple flowers

Red campion
30-70 cm; woods
Apr-Sep

Shining crane's-bill
10-30 cm; limestone rocks
May-Aug

Herb-robert
10-30 cm; woods, rocks
Apr-Sep

Wild thyme
3-10 cm; grassland, rocks
May-Aug

Water mint
15-40 cm; wet places
Jul-Oct

Selfheal
5-15 cm; grassland
Jun-Sep

Bitter-vetch
15-30 cm; grassland
May-Jul

Cuckooflower
15-20 cm; damp grassland
Apr-Jun

Bloody crane's-bill
10-40 cm; limestone grassland,
rocks
Jul-Aug

Giant bellfower
60-100 cm; grassland, woods
Jul-Aug

Common butterwort
5-15 cm; bogs and fens, damp
grassland
May-Jul

Common dog-violet
5-20 cm; grassland, woods
Apr-May

Harebell
10-25 cm; grassland, rocks
Jul-Sep

Ground-ivy
7-15 cm; grassland, woods
Apr-May

Field scabious
20-50 cm; grassland
Jul-Sep

Germander speedwell
10-20 cm; grassland, woods
Apr-Jul

Bugle
10-25 cm; grassland, woods
Apr-Jun

Ivy-leaved toadflax
5-15 cm; rocks
May-Aug

Blue or red flowers

Meadow crane's-bill
25-60 cm; grassland
Jun-Aug

Wood crane's-bill
25-50 cm; grassland, woods
Jun-Aug

Bluebell
20-35 cm; woods
Apr-Jun

Tufted vetch
30-60 cm; grassland
Jun-Aug

Hedge woundwort
30-60 cm; woods
Jul-Sep

Marsh cinquefoil
20-40 cm; wet places
Jun-Jul

Red clover
10-30 cm; grassland
Jun-Sep

Ramsons
15-40 cm; woods
Apr-May

Eyebright
5-15 cm; grassland
Jul-Sep

Rue-leaved Saxifrage
4-15 cm; rocks
May-Jun

Yarrow
15-35 cm; grassland
Jun-Sep

Wood anemone
10-20 cm; woods
Apr-May

Round-leaved sundew
5-15 cm; bogs
Jun-Aug

Wild strawberry
5-25 cm; limestone grassland,
woods
Apr-Jul

Hoary plantain
10-30 cm; limestone grassland
May-Aug

Woodruff
15-25 cm; limestone woodland
May-Jun

Dropwort
10-40 cm; limestone grassland
May-Aug

White flowers

Garlic mustard
20-60 cm; woods
Apr-Jun

Lesser stitchwort
15-35 cm; acid grassland, woods
May-Jul

Greater stitchwort
15-45 cm; grassland, woods
Apr-June

White campion
30-70 cm; grassland, woods
May-Sep

Oxeye daisy
20-60 cm; grassland
May-Aug

Bogbean
10-30 cm; bogs, fens, ponds
Jun-Jul

Snowdrop
15-20 cm; woods
Feb-Mar

Water-cress
20-35 cm; streams
May-Sep

Bird cherry
3-15 m; woods
May

Hawthorn
2-10 m; field edges, woods
May-Jun

Herb-paris
15-30 cm; limestone woods
May-July

Common cottongrass
20-35 cm; bogs
May-Jun

Blue moor-grass
15-35 cm; limestone grassland,
limestone rocks
May-Aug

Juniper
1-6 m; upland areas on
limestone

Brittle bladder-fern
To 25 cm; limestone rocks

Wall-rue
To 20 cm; limestone rocks

Maidenhair spleenwort
To 40 cm; rocks

Green spleenwort
To 15 cm; limestone rocks

Hard fern
To 50 cm; grassland, acid woods,
moors

Hart's-tongue
To 50 cm; woods, damp rocks

Further reading and contact addresses

Recommended identification guides

Rose, F. (1981) *The wild flower key*. London: Frederick Warne.

Rose, F. (1989) *Grasses, sedges, rushes and ferns of the British Isles and north-western Europe*. London: Viking.

Other useful books

Drewwitt, A. (1991) *The vegetation of the Yorkshire Dales National Park*. Grassington: Yorkshire Dales National Park.

The Field Studies Council produce a number of simple and very useful identification charts, including:

Grasses; Grassland plants; Plants common on the moorlands; Woodland plants

Maps

Ordnance Survey 1:25,000 scale
EXPLORER OL30 Yorkshire Dales Northern/Central Area
EXPLORER OL32 Yorkshire Dales Southern/Western Area
www.ordnancesurvey.co.uk

Contact addresses

English Nature (Leyburn Office)
Asquith House
Leyburn Business Park
Harmby Road
LEYBURN
DL8 5QA
Tel. 01969 623447
www.english-nature.org.uk

Field Studies Council
Preston Montford
SHREWSBURY
SY4 1HW
Tel. 01743 852140
www.field-studies-council.org

Plantlife
21 Elizabeth Street
LONDON
SW1W 9RP
Tel. 020 7808 0100
www.plantlife.org.uk

Yorkshire Dales National Park
Colvend
Hebden Road
Grassington
SKIPTON
N Yorks
BD23 5LB
Tel. 01756 752748
www.yorkshiredales.org.uk

The Woodland Trust
Autumn Park
GRANTHAM
Lincolnshire
NG31 6LL
Tel. 01476 581111
www.woodland-trust.org.uk

Yorkshire Wildlife Trust
10 Toft Green
YORK
YO1 6JT
Tel. 01904 659570
www.yorkshire-wildlife-trust.org.uk

THE COUNTRY CODE

- Enjoy the countryside and respect its life and work
- Guard against all risk of fire
- Fasten all gates
- Keep your dogs under close control
- Keep to public paths across farmland
- Use gates and stiles to cross fences, hedges and walls
- Leave livestock, crops and machinery alone
- Take your litter home
- Help to keep all water clean
- Protect wildlife, plants and trees
- Take special care on country roads
- Make no unnecessary noise

PLANT INDEX

Page references in **bold** refer to plant photographs

PLANT INDEX

Page references in **bold** refer to plant photographs

PLANT INDEX Page references in **bold** refer to plant photographs

The authors

Wife and husband team Amanda and Brin Best met while studying ecology and environmental science at the University of East Anglia. After graduating they took part in award-winning research expeditions to the Ecuadorian rainforests, then returned to the UK to live and work in Yorkshire. They have always shared a love of natural history, and became captivated by the flora and landscape of the Yorkshire Dales, which they have explored from their home in Wharfedale for the last ten years.

Amanda Best has worked as a professional ecologist for the Environment Agency since its formation in 1996. Before this, she was a conservation officer for the National Rivers' Authority. She is a member of the Institute of Ecology and Environmental Management and currently serves as Environment Secretary for the Wharfedale Naturalists' Society.

Brin Best works both as an education consultant and a writer, and has written a number of books on environmental issues. Prior to this he worked in schools, including four years as Head of Geography at Settle High School. He is a Fellow of the Royal Geographical Society and was awarded a Millennium Fellowship for his pioneering work with young people on the environment.

Acknowledgements

Angus McNab kindly allowed us to use the photograph of him in a Ribblesdale hay meadow (p.46). We thank Karen Broom for her photograph of us both which appears on this page.

We would like to thank our relatives and friends who have accompanied us on the walks and helped us to find additional species.

Tony Thomas and Adrian Pickles provided valuable additional information about Malham Tarn, and Roger Hardingham encouraged us at every stage of the production process.

Map legend

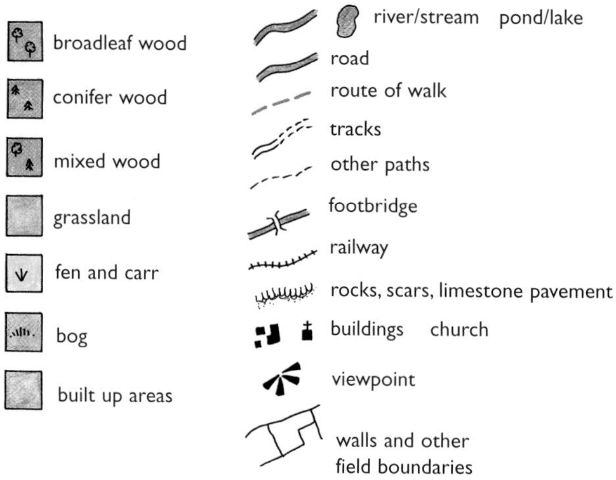

broadleaf wood

conifer wood

mixed wood

grassland

fen and carr

bog

built up areas

river/stream   pond/lake

road

route of walk

tracks

other paths

footbridge

railway

rocks, scars, limestone pavement

buildings   church

viewpoint

walls and other
field boundaries

NOTES